The Es

TRIUMPH
STAG
1970 to 1977

Your marque experts:
Norm Mort & Tony Fox
Photography by Andrew Mort

VELOCE PUBLISHING
THE PUBLISHER OF FINE AUTOMOTIVE BOOKS

www.veloce.co.uk

First published in February 2009. Reprinted in December 2017 by Veloce Publishing Limited, Veloce House, Parkway Farm Business Park, Middle
Farm Way, Poundbury, Dorchester, Dorset, DT1 3AR, England. Fax 01305 250479/info@veloce.co.uk/www.veloce.co.uk or www.velocebooks.com.
ISBN: 978-1-787112-80-3 UPC: 6-36847-01280-9
British Library Cataloguing in Publication Data – A catalogue record for this book is available from the British Library. Typesetting, design and page
make-up all by Veloce Publishing Ltd on Apple Mac. Printed and bound by CPI Group (UK) Ltd, Croydon, CR0 4YY.

Introduction
With the introduction of the TR series in 1952, the Triumph nameplate came to the forefront of the world's sports car market. Sporting saloons evolved, as did Triumph's popular TR, Spitfire and GT6 models. This eventually led to the development of the more powerful, up-market Stag.

Introduced as a 1970 model in the Triumph range, the grand touring 4-seater, V8 Stag was a completely new concept for the marque.

Introduced in 1970, the production Triumph Stag combined the smoothness and performance of a 145bhp (127bhp in North America – NA) SOHC V8 engine, in a stylish, 2+2 model, Italian coachwork design for either GT, or open grand touring. The long list of standard features included synchromesh 4-speed transmission with overdrive (or an optional Borg Warner 3-speed automatic), fully independent suspension, power assisted rack-and-pinion steering, power windows, vacuum servo brakes with front discs, and a T-brace roll bar. All new was the 3.0L V8 engine, based on the four-cylinder units developed in cooperation with Saab.

Today, with all the major problems having been largely resolved, owning a Triumph Stag can be a very rewarding experience. Keen enthusiasts and excellent club support means there's always help nearby.

In production terms, most of the difficulties were resolved by the mid-1970s, yet the earlier Stags tend to be favoured by some because the majority of cars have been upgraded over the past three decades, appear to have a better build quality, and were more commonly fitted with a manual transmission. Prices vary considerably, though, and, although, spares are generally plentiful, the cost of restoration can easily outstrip the current market value.

Many of the UK and US collector car magazines, such as *Classic Cars* in the UK and *Sports Car Market* in the US, contain price guide information. Similar magazines are offered in other countries, too, but all contain values based on the average price, or an individual car.

Demand for the Triumph Stag has been steadily increasing, and this book is an indispensable tool for pre-inspection, purchase and future reference. The handy pocket-sized *Essential Buyer's Guide* is designed to assist the potential owner to find the right car at the right price. This guide explains every aspect of purchasing a Triumph Stag, and is designed to answer all questions, whether you're seeking to purchase a fully restored example, a project car, a well cared for original, or a modified/updated version. To help you make a confident purchase the book contains essential costing data, step-by-step inspection techniques, and a unique points system designed to help you evaluate any Stag.

The following pages include a wealth of information, from vital statistics to the optional factory equipment offered, as well as highlighting many of the 'fixes and upgrades' available to ensure you enjoy your Triumph Stag for years to come.

Thanks

Andrew Mort's keen eye was responsible for virtually all the photographs in this book. Thanks also to Stag owners Albert Koo, Roger Tipple, Patrick Rushe, Michael Coffey and Tony Fox (Jr).

Norm Mort & Tony Fox
Ontario, Canada

The Triumph Stag changed little in appearance throughout its production.

Contents

The Essential Buyer's Guide™ currency
At the time of publication a BG unit of currency "●" equals approximately £1.00/US$1.32/Euro 1.11. Please adjust to suit current exchange rates.

1 Is it the right car for you?
– marriage guidance

Tall and short drivers
The Stag is surprisingly roomy for front seat occupants, even those over 72in/182.88cm, with good cabin width.

Weight of controls
Excellent ergonomics with power steering, windows and brakes. The manual transmission has a positive feel and a wide throw. Steering column-mounted switches operate the wipers, indicators, horn, lights, and ignition.

Will it fit in the garage?
Length: 173.7in/441.1cm
Width: 63.5in/161.3cm

Interior space
Front seats are adjustable fore and aft, as are the seat and squab angles. Rear seating for children, or occasional use for adults. The steering column can also be adjusted; up and down and telescopically.

Luggage capacity
There is luggage space for two medium-size suitcases, with some space around the spare wheel. Additional storage is available in the soft top storage well and rear seat area. A

The Triumph Stag offers sporting flair with family seating, making it a very attractive collectable.

glovebox and door pockets provide space for small items.

Running costs
Moderate, with strict regular maintenance being required, but nothing exceptional. Expect 24-28mpg (10-11.8L/100km).

Usability
Suitable for everyday driving as the Stag easily keeps up with modern traffic.

Parts availability
Excellent! Pretty well everything available from UK suppliers, but more limited in North America.

Parts cost
See chapter 2 for details on parts.

Insurance group
Reasonable premiums are available through a club scheme or speciality insurance. Get an appraisal and 'agreed value' policy.

Investment potential
Moderate. Prices have not risen significantly yet, but could very well do as families and drivers mature and are drawn to the appeal of the Stag's virtues. Buy the best you can afford as it's ultimately less expensive.

Brooklands Green was a 1977 model year only colour. The Stag pictured here was the last one off the production line. During the Stag's lifetime, 33 different colours were offered. (Courtesy Tony Fox)

Foibles
Few today, but needs regular maintenance.

Plus points
Extremely comfortable long distance driver with good handling, wonderful V8 sound and great club support.

Minus points
Few once sorted, but needs careful servicing to keep reliability at peak.

Alternatives
Mercedes-Benz SL & SLC
Alfa-Romeo 2000GTV & Alfetta GT
Reliant Scimitar GTC
Peugeot 504 Cabriolet

2 Cost considerations
– affordable, or a money pit?

Parts supply for the Stag today is excellent, with several major suppliers in the UK. Supplies in North America are more limited, but improving all the time, with currently one dedicated supplier. Prices are very reasonable when compared to modern cars. The main, essential servicing costs are: changing the engine oil every 3000 miles, and replacing the antifreeze every two years. Timing chains should be checked for wear after 30,000 miles.

(Prices exclude taxes)

Mechanical parts
Clutch ●x105
Front brake discs, each ●x31
Front brake pads, set ●x9
Exhaust system, mild steel ●x249
Radiator, exchange ●x38
Coolant hoses, set ●x43
Alternator, exchange ●x94
Starter, exchange ●x82
Distributor ●x134
Front shock absorbers ●x31
Rear shock absorbers ●x19
Brake servo ●x145
Brake master cylinder ●x133
Rear brake shoes, set ●x17
Clutch master cylinder ●x58
Clutch slave cylinder ●x18
Cylinder head gasket ●x32
Engine gasket set, complete ●x43
Reconditioned engine complete
    ●x2000 up
Gearbox rebuild, 4-speed overdrive
    ●x600

Gearbox rebuild, BW auto ●x420
Overdrive rebuild ●x322
Differential assembly rebuild ●x344
Propeller shaft, new ●x113
Fuel tank, new x245
Fuel pump ●x70
Carburetor rebuild kit ●x66

Body
Front wing ●x213
Rocker/sills ●x93
Door panel ●x59
Bonnet ●x200
Windscreen ●x113

Interior
Seat cover kit, complete, front ●x305
Seat cover kit, complete, rear ●x169
Carpet set ●x144 up
Soft top, mohair ●x302 up

Often the most costly repairs involve the various potential maladies concerning cooling and the 3.0L V8.

An uninstalled replacement black mohair soft top will cost in the region of ●x302 plus. The MkI tops had rear quarter lights, whereas the MkII models had only the rear window and, thus, poorer rearward visibility.

Hard-to-find parts

A few parts specific to the Federal cars are getting hard to find, such as the different Stag emblem on the rear wing. Air-conditioning components are scarce, too. The internet has been a big bonus to enthusiasts when looking for replacement parts, both new and used. The Tooling Fund of the Stag Owners' Club has proved invaluable in the sourcing and funding of replacement parts in many instances, particularly body panels, which require a big outlay for press tooling.

3 Living with a Stag
– will you get along together?

The original concept car was styled by Michelotti as a European show car in 1966, based on a 2000 saloon supplied by Triumph preceding the formation of British Leyland. The prototype was so well liked by Triumph's Director of Engineering, Harry Webster, that he insisted on taking the car back to Coventry, to be considered for production by the Triumph Board of Directors.

The Stag nomenclature came into the Triumph range as the prototype's code name and, ultimately, Marketing approved and adopted the model name when launched.

An early MkI Stag can be quickly recognised by its clean flanks, although many owners have since applied rub strips along the side.

Earmarked for production, over the ensuing four years the design was further developed by Triumph. The 2000 sedan was widened and stiffened. The grille became a series of simple chrome bars that abandoned Michelotti's original sliding cover arrangement, while the front running/indicators and the taillights were both sunken and V-ed: all of which provided the Stag with a smoother appearance, fore and aft.

Although the Stag was first onto the drawing board, the Michelotti-styled 2000 saloon MkII, the Spitfire MkIV, and the GT6 MkIII all shared its styling cues, and appeared in 1969 and 1970.

Mechanically, the Stag utilised the front suspension, steering, rear suspension, gearbox, rear axle and brakes of the 2000, with only minor modifications.

The 2+2 Stag's most distinctive feature was its T-bar roof, which was originally designed for structural integrity, and to meet potential American convertible safety regulations. Initially, a hefty hardtop that clipped into position with four latches and a spring-loaded latch at the rear was optional. Later, these all-weather tops became standard equipment.

When removed, the manual cloth top was neatly hidden under a padded metal tonneau, virtually identical to that of the Mercedes-Benz 280SL. This top was easily pulled up or down, over the fixed rollover T-brace roll cage. Despite the fact that the T-brace did little for the Stag's overall aesthetics, from a safety viewpoint it was an excellent design.

Although comfortable, the accommodation with its vinyl coverings was viewed as being only semi-luxurious, considering the Stag's retail price. Many thought the Stag's introductory price was expensive for a Triumph, with the hardtop/soft top version listed at £2107 (US$5805), or just $1200 lower than a Jaguar V12 XKE.

A vinyl interior was always offered in the Stag, but, overall, in appearance and comfort, it was quite luxurious.

Rushed into production, the new 3.0L V8 proved troublesome. This engine became the Stag's Achilles heel, in part due to cooling problems and warping heads, as well as other niggling problems that included bearing, crankshaft and timing chain maladies. Also typical for the 1970s were corrosion woes.

Over the next seven years, many factory fixes, improvements, and aftermarket alternatives were instigated. Those enthusiasts who adapted to the various maladies of the Stag went on to become die-hard fans. Now, nearly forty years later, the problems that once plagued the Stag have all but been solved. Its styling has aged well, with the subtle nuances of its Italianesque lines being admired by more and more enthusiasts; which accounts for the fact that more than fifty per cent of Triumph Stag production survives today.

Today, the choice of motoring, either in manual convertible or hardtop GT form, is very appealing. A Stag with its hardtop in place is as snug and solid as any coupé. Power windows and hinged rear vents provide more than adequate ventilation in warm climates, while the optional air-conditioning allows for comfortable touring on the hottest days. The substantial manual cloth top is easy to operate and fits snugly in place. Additionally, when the top is down, the Stag's distinctive fixed

Stag Owners' Club Tooling Fund Ltd is the moving force that endeavours to ensure various hard-to-get bits, body panels and engine heads are available to keep your Stag on the road.

window frames and unique T-brace roll cage allow for open motoring with minimal buffeting.

The Stag's once troublesome V8 has been sorted and improved upon over the years. If maintained properly, the torque of the V8 will provide good, smooth performance and reasonable fuel economy, along with an appealing exhaust burble, for at least 100,000 miles (169,930km). Front power-assisted disc brakes and rear drums offer adequate stopping power, even by today's standards.

Parts are widely available, thanks to strong club support and marque suppliers. In fact, like many of the British sporting cars, parts are easier to obtain today than when the cars were new. The common problem areas have all been well addressed, so these items are commonly stocked. Other parts can be ordered or found through the clubs.

The Triumph Stag appears to be more popular today, as a collector car, than it was when first sold. The side stripes and black rear fascia panel (ultimately dropped in 1975), were two of the most noticeable appearance changes on the MkII.

As a stylish and practical driving collectable the Stag can be very satisfying, as long as you choose the correct example. As always, buy the best you can afford, as it is often far less expensive in the long run.

Thus, the Triumph Stag has become a very viable and affordable collector's car that allows an enthusiast to cover great distances quickly and safely, while providing relaxed accommodation for the entire family.

4 Relative values
– which model for you?

Unlike many car models, the Triumph Stag did not change dramatically in appearance and specification over its seven year production span from 1970-1977. Yet, that is not to say that every year is the same or has the same market value. Additionally, British and European Stag models differed considerably from those exported to the United States (commonly referred to as Federal Cars). Early 1971-1973 Stags are referred to as Mkl cars, and the 1973-1977 designated Mkll. This, however, was not the official factory designation, but does allow owners to differentiate the major design split in specification. Some owners prefer the earlier, cleaner looking Mkl Stag, while others favour the later improved Mkll versions.

Early Stags built before 1975 had more problems than the later Mkll versions. In simple terms, the earlier the model year, the greater the number of problem areas that need to be checked.

Early Stag models built from 1970-1975 were prone to numerous problems, but improved with each consecutive year. Fortunately, those 'problem areas' specific to the Stag have long been identified, and there are 'fixes' available.

Now, over three decades later, some Stags on the market may have had these

In very original Stags, some of these problems have yet to surface. These areas of concern must be carefully scrutinised in the Stag you are considering. The addition of an electric fan is perhaps an indication that earlier cooling problems have been addressed.

areas previously attended to, others ignored or subjected to a quick fix rather than being fully resolved.

A Stag in roadworthy and useable condition sells for roughly ●x4000-●x6000 at the time of writing, while a concours condition Stag is priced in the ●x10,000-●x12,000 range. A rough, but very restorable, Stag has a market value in the ●x2000 range.

A common quick fix was the installation of a Buick V6 in North America, or a Rover 3.5L V8 or Ford V6 in Britain. Minor engine compartment modifications were necessary for both.

Owners have never tended to change the exterior appearance of the Stag, but what lies under the hood could be very different. This Stag appears stock, but is powered by a 3.8L V6, which reduces its value.

Stag buyers should also note that there are many specification differences between British, European and North American Stags. Stags have been privately imported over the years. A right-hand Stag in North America, naturally, has a lower value. The VIN on the inside door jamb should be checked on these Stags to ensure they have been imported legally.

Desirable optional equipment, such as wire wheels and a hardtop, will increase the value of your Stag.

A total of 25,939 Stags were built between 1970 and 1977, with only 2871 officially imported into the US between 1971 and 1973.

Rare Stags include this one of three fastbacks, only one of which is known to survive; a number of AWD Stags equipped with Ferguson Formula (FF) units (two known); a post-production 1980s Tickford Stag, and a pickup version.

5 Before you view
– be well informed

To avoid a wasted journey, and the disappointment of finding that the Stag does not match your expectations, it will help if you're very clear about what questions you want to ask before you pick up the telephone. Some of these points might appear basic but, when you're excited about the prospect of buying your dream classic, it's amazing how some of the most obvious things slip the mind. Also check the current values of the model you are interested in in classic car magazines, which give both a price guide and auction results.

Where is the Stag?
Is it going to be worth travelling to the next county/state, or even across a border? A locally advertised Stag, although it may not sound very interesting, can add to your knowledge for very little effort, so make a visit – it might even be in better condition than expected.

Dealer or private sale?
Establish early on if the Stag is being sold by its owner or by a trader. A private owner should have all the history, so don't be afraid to ask detailed questions. A dealer may have more limited knowledge of a car's history, but should have some documentation. A dealer may offer a warranty/guarantee (ask for a printed copy) and finance.

Cost of collection and delivery
A dealer may well be used to quoting for delivery by car transporter. A private owner may agree to meet you halfway, but only agree to this after you have seen the Stag at the vendor's address to validate the documents. Conversely, you could meet halfway and agree the sale but insist on meeting at the vendor's address for the handover.

Reason for sale
Do make this one of the first questions. Why is the Stag being sold and how long has it been with the current owner? How many previous owners?

View – when and where?
It is always preferable to view at the vendor's home or business premises. In the case of a private sale, the Stag's documentation should tally with the vendor's name and address. Arrange to view only in daylight and avoid a wet day. Most cars look better in poor light or when wet.

Left-hand drive to right-hand drive?
If a steering conversion is required (NA versus Britain) it can only reduce the value, and it may well be that other aspects of the car still reflect the specification for a foreign market. In the case of the Triumph Stag the differences are not huge or insurmountable, but certain conversions may be required by law. Some drivers feel uncomfortable driving a vehicle with the steering 'on the other side.'

There have been a few Stag 'specials' constructed: Three fastback coupés were constructed by the factory, and privately 'Tickford' versions and a pickup have been built.

Condition (body/chassis/interior/mechanicals)?
Ask for an honest appraisal of the Stag's condition. Ask specifically about some of the check items described in chapter 7.

All original specification?
A Stag with original equipment is invariably of higher value than a customised version.

Matching data/legal ownership
Do VIN/chassis, engine numbers and registration plate match the official registration document? Is the owner's name and address recorded in the official registration documents?

For those countries that require an annual test of roadworthiness, does the Stag have a document showing it complies (an MoT certificate in the UK, which can be verified on 0300 123 9000 or gov.uk/check-mot-status)? If a smog/emissions certificate is mandatory, does the car have one?

If required, does the Stag carry a current road fund licence/licence plate tag?

Does the vendor own the car outright? Money might be owed to a finance company or bank: the Stag could even be stolen. Several organisations will supply the data on ownership, based on the car's registration plate number, for a fee. Such companies can often also tell you whether the Stag has been 'written off' by an insurance company. In the UK these organisations can supply vehicle data:

DVSA 0300 123 9000
HPI 0845 300 8905
AA 0344 209 0754
DVLA 0844 306 9203
RAC 0800 015 6000
Other countries will have similar organisations.

Unleaded fuel?
If necessary, has the car been modified to run on unleaded fuel?

Insurance
Check with your existing insurer before setting out, your current policy might not cover you to drive the car if you do purchase it.

How can you pay?
A cheque will take several days to clear and the seller may prefer to sell to a cash buyer. However, a banker's draft (a cheque issued by a bank) is as good as cash, but safer, so contact your own bank and become familiar with the formalities that are necessary to obtain one.

Buying at auction?
If the intention is to buy at auction see chapter 10 for further advice.

Professional vehicle checks
There are often marque/model specialists who will undertake professional examination of a vehicle on your behalf. Owners' clubs will be able to put you in touch with such specialists.

Other organisations that will carry out a general professional check in the UK are:

AA 0800 056 8040 (motoring organisation with vehicle inspectors)
RAC 0330 159 0720 (motoring organisation with vehicle inspectors)
Other countries will have similar organisations.

6 Inspection equipment
– these items will really help

This book
Reading glasses (if you need them for close work)
Magnet (not powerful, a fridge magnet is ideal)
Flashlight
Probe (a small screwdriver works very well)
Overalls
Mirror on a stick
Digital camera
A friend, preferably a knowledgeable enthusiast

Before you rush out of the door, gather together a few items that will help as you work your way around the proposed Stag. This book is designed to be your guide at every step, so take it along and use the check boxes in chapter 9 to help you assess each area of the car you're interested in. Don't be afraid to let the seller see you using it.

Take your reading glasses if you need them to read documents and make close-up inspections.

A magnet will help you check if the car is full of filler, or has fibreglass panels. Use the magnet to sample bodywork areas all around the car, but be careful not to damage the paintwork. Expect to find a little filler here and there, but not whole panels. There's nothing wrong with fibreglass panels, but a purist might want the car to be as original as possible.

A flashlight with fresh batteries will be useful for peering into the wheelarches and under the Stag.

A small blunt screwdriver can be used – with care – as a probe, particularly in the wheelarches and on the underside. With this you should be able to check an area of severe corrosion, but be careful – if it's really bad the screwdriver might go right through the metal!

Be prepared to get dirty. Take along a pair of overalls, if you have them. Fixing a mirror at an angle on the end of a stick may seem odd, but you'll probably need it to check the condition of the underside of the Stag. It will also help you to peer into some of the important crevices. You can also use it, together with the flashlight, along the underside of the sills and on the floor.

If you have the use of a digital camera, take it along so that later you can study some areas of the car more closely. Take a picture of any part of the car that causes you concern, and seek a friend's opinion.

Ideally, have a friend or knowledgeable enthusiast accompany you: a second opinion is always valuable.

The bare minimum inspection kit.

Only buy a car from an individual who can prove that they are the person named in the car's registration document (V5C in the UK) and, preferably, at the address shown in the document. Also check that the VIN or chassis number/frame and engine numbers of the car match the numbers in the registration document, as many cars are modified the years to disguise them as later models, or for more ominous reasons. This plate is located on the left side door jamb on the B-post. UK cars don't have a cross-reference plate under the bonnet, whereas North American Stags have a matching plate just inside the windscreen, attached to the A-pillar.

A Stag fitted with its original numbers and matching Triumph 3.0-litre V8 engine is preferable, but not essential as long as it is the proper Triumph unit. The engine number is stamped into the block near the distributor. Ask whether a British Motor Heritage certificate, to confirm the numbers and the build date, has been acquired.

Exterior
The majority of Stag enthusiasts are looking for a car that is immediately useable or better, rather than an example requiring total restoration. Thus, first impressions on viewing the Stag are very important. A simple point, but an important one, is to ensure that the Stag is complete. Adding missing parts or accessories can be very costly, regardless of how small and incidental they seem.

Check carefully that the paint is not peeling, fading, or full of scratches, scrapes and rust blemishes.

Next, is the paint presentable or is it peeling, fading, or full of scratches, scrapes and rust blemishes, from one end to the other? At the same time, be suspicious of freshly-applied paint. The seller should have a receipt to prove that professional repairs and paintwork were undertaken. A quick paint re-spray of the body, fresh

bumpers, new carpet sets and some basic paint and detailing under the hood does not make a 'restored' Stag. Are there dents or areas of obvious rusting? Is all the chrome decent and present, or are pieces of trim missing?

Replacing chrome bumpers and trim, bodywork and paint quickly adds up, and it may be far cheaper to buy a slightly better-looking Stag at only slightly more money.

The cost of replacing chrome bumpers and trim, bodywork and paint soon adds up, and could put your Stag project over-budget very quickly.

A small magnet moved over the body will help locate areas that contain filler, indicating a quick fix.

Any Stag that has been stored for years and is still covered in dust and dirt should not be considered until the owner has washed the car so you can see what you are considering buying. A layer of dirt will hide a multitude of problems. Even older restorations, if improperly stored for five or ten years, could require a complete rebuild. Rust from dampness, mice, and seizing from lack of use, can quickly transform a former concours winner into a parts car.

Check all seams for rust.

Quite often, careless use of the soft and hardtops can lead to scratches at the chrome-plated header rail latching points and rear centre latching location, not to mention the surrounding paintwork. Check the rear B-pillar stainless trim, too. Careless removal and fitment of the hardtop can make deep grooves here.

The phrase 'all that glitters is *not* gold' should be borne in mind when buying any classic car, and is particularly relevant when buying a Triumph Stag.

The frame components and entire underside of the unibody design are all important in a Stag. There are also numerous essential areas.

Examine the rear wings where they meet the lower sills. Is there bubbling or rusting at the seam? For that matter, make sure that the seam is still there and not covered up with filler.

Check for rust on the underside of the rearmost lip of the boot lid, and the rear shock absorber mounts in the soft top well. It is typical to find rust in any or all of the wheelarch flanges.

The frame members are part of the unibody structure and important in the overall integrity of the Stag. In particular, check for rust where the floor meets the outer sills.

Another rare, but a walk away problem with the Stag, is the failure of the outrigger subframe near the rear suspension. The ends tend to crack, rust and break. This problem often doesn't manifest itself until separation of the end flange.

Other rust areas to check include the floors under the rear seat cushions, where water can accumulate, the leading edge of the bonnet, the A-posts where the doors hinge – both at the base where they meet the sills and higher up into the windshield support frame.

If the Stag comes with a hardtop, check if the leading edge is rusty.

Examine all the window glass carefully for breaks, cracks, delamination, and scratches. The windscreen should be cleaned thoroughly to check for wiper blade scratches, stone chips, or excessive pitting. Likewise, all other glass, mirrors, lamps and lenses need careful scrutiny for damage.

The windscreen, and all other glass, mirrors, lamps and lenses, need careful scrutiny to check for damage.

Although a relatively inexpensive interior to replace, careful scrutiny of the dash, seats, carpets and panels will help you decide just how much work, as well as money, will be required to remedy problems.

Interior

Although the Stag was never known to be produced with a leather interior, its vinyl interior and carpets are still a substantial replacement cost. Keep in mind that the vinyl on the seats and panels, although appearing to be excellent, will have to be removed to replace interior foam and padding. Often the foam in the seats has reached the stage where it crumbles. Signs of foam deterioration can be found under the seats, looking like small piles of sawdust, while the vinyl itself will be loose fitting and wrinkled. You'll also note there may be little support. Sit in both the passenger seat and driver's seat, as the base support diaphragms often crack and lose their support. While refinishing the dash or replacing any instruments is no hardship, a cracked dash is expensive to replace.

Turn on the ignition, lights, sound the horn, try the indicators and the radio to see if everything electrical is working.

Check that all the controls, handles, and bits of trim are still fitted and in good condition. Although not overly expensive, these small pieces add up quickly, and every missing part is an added expense.

Examine the board trim panels on the doors, side and kick panels to ensure these have not become warped due to moisture.

A new carpet kit is relatively inexpensive, but unless you can install it yourself the cost will be three times as much. Lift the carpets in the footwells to see if the floor is rotting. Over the years, to keep the Stag on the road, the floors may have been patched with metal and then tarred. Sometimes these patches were just large sheets of metal screwed into place. Professionally repaired floors, welded into place, should not deter you from buying.

If the hardtop is fitted, check the headliner and then ask if the owner will remove it, so you can check the condition of the cloth top.

If the soft top is up, check it for small tears, wear on corners, fading, and scratches on the rear window. Try folding it to see if the top bows fold easily and properly, and flat enough for the rear tonneau panel to be fastened and conceal it. Make sure none of the elements of the frame are missing or bent. Additionally, the header rail must be able to float at the hinge on either side; a welded or seized joint will not last. Make sure the rear window can be unzipped easily. The MkI Stag featured rear quarter lights that tended to get scratched and damaged when folded.

The battery tray is always prone to rust as water tends to get trapped between the battery and metal framework. Also check to see if the battery clamp is securely in place and not missing. Unfortunately, it's not easy to remove the battery to check this as you need to place the power steering pump to one side. It's not necessary to disconnect the pump, but rather just move it aside to allow clearance for the battery to be removed.

If the Stag is in running condition, look under the dash before trying to start the car. If there appears to be wiring problems it's best to walk away. Any car with burnt or bodged wiring can be a nightmare that often is solved only by rewiring the entire vehicle.

If running, upon switching on the ignition you should be faced with warning lights. The low fuel warning light may come on even though there is a quarter of a tank of fuel remaining. This is quite normal, but make sure no other warning lights remain on after starting.

Check that the heater fan is working on both speeds, and that the windscreen wipers operate correctly.

Make sure all the electrical functions are working properly. The indicator lights and four-way flashers can be slow, or even stop, at engine idle. This can be easily rectified by fitting an inexpensive, heavy-duty flasher unit.

The power windows may also be quite slow if operated without the engine running, so try them again later with it running and see if there is an improvement. Stag clocks are notorious for failing, but this may not be important to you. A number of owners have replaced the clock with an oil pressure gauge, and rely on a modern radio fitted with a digital readout for timekeeping.

Mechanicals

A common problem is for the starter to simply click and not turn the engine. Usually, this means a replacement is in order, although it could just be a poor ground.

If the engine is the original Triumph 3.0L design, pay particular attention to the sound of the timing chains, especially when starting the engine. Worn timing chains will rattle on start up, but may quieten after a few seconds. This means the chains need replacing soon. If there is a continuous rattle while running, the chains are well past their due date for a change. Should the timing chains either snap or jump a tooth, the valves will touch the pistons, and this means a major repair job. The heads must then come off and be repaired and the valves will need to be replaced. (This is not unique to the Stag engine, but is a factor to take into consideration.)

No production Stag models were fitted with an oil pressure gauge, but many have since been so equipped. If you are lucky enough to have an oil pressure gauge on the car you are examining, then an assessment is possible. The Stag never enjoyed a particularly high pressure system, and if you get a reading of 50psi hot at highway speeds, then consider that good. Even 45psi is tolerable, but a factor to bear in mind. Idle, hot of course, will drop to 20 or 15psi. Anything lower than these numbers should be considered carefully before making a decision to purchase. Some engines have been fitted with high output pumps from the Saab unit which can produce pressures above 60psi. Opinion is divided on this, as some feel it will place undue strain on the timing chains.

If you adore the looks and character of the Stag and care less about the engine, as long as it runs, then a Rover V8, Ford or Buick V6 engine should not upset you, as long as the conversion has been done properly and professionally. Make sure that a lighter engine has been compensated for with the necessary revisions to the front suspension. In other words, does the front end sit high due to a lightweight engine

Pay attention when starting the engine! Worn timing chains will rattle on start up, but may quieten after a few seconds. This means the chains need replacing soon.

substitution? There are some Stag owners that want economical, more reliable motoring, and these engines certainly provide that, with little loss of performance, handling or economy. In some areas, such as acceleration, fuel economy, etc., these conversions may actually be better than a factory V8 original, but don't kid yourself, the market value for these cars is on average a third to half in comparison. It should also be noted that to retrofit an original engine is an extremely expensive conversion. Not only must you source all the conversion parts, but it would be foolhardy to fit an engine that had not been completely rebuilt. This, too, adds considerably to the ultimate cost of making your Stag drivable.

If the Stag you are considering does not have its original Triumph 3.0L V8, but has been fitted with a replacement Triumph unit, there is little difference in value. It is more important that the 3.0L is running well and has had the various recommended improvements.

Regardless of what powerplant you find under the bonnet, ask the vendor to start the engine while you keep an eye on the exhaust pipes. The motor should fire-up immediately, especially if the owner had already pulled it out of the garage. At start up, listen carefully for timing chain rattle. If the owner claims it runs but the battery is dead, this is where the spare battery you brought along comes in handy. If the exhaust has a blue haze after more than a few seconds then there is valve, piston or ring wear, particularly if it increases when the engine is revved. Check the underside for exhaust leaks, and then take a look at the engine. Is it running smoothly and quietly as it idles? Are there any knocks, rattles or changes in revs? If you can't hear the engine run – walk away.

Check under the Stag, looking for oil, fuel or other fluid leaks, and at how much rust is on the brake and fuel lines, fuel tank and brakes.

Finally, check the overall stance of the car. Does it sit low/high over the front or rear springs; does it lean to one side, or sag in the middle? Test the shocks by pushing on each wing. There should be good resistance and no bounce after the push to indicate the shocks are not worn.

Walk away or stay?
Having checked the body for corrosion, the overall condition of the interior, looked under the bonnet and in the boot, made a cursory inspection of the chassis and

listened to the engine run, you should have a good idea if this is the Stag you are looking for, and if the price reflects its general condition. Don't underestimate the time and money necessary to make this Stag into the car you want. If you have little time, keep in mind that even minor restoration work consumes countless hours and weekends you might not have available.

Still, if this Stag is a good buy then it will sell fairly quickly. Saying you'll think about it until next week may mean you lose the opportunity of buying a Stag perfect for your needs and budget. So, if it looks promising, go on to do a more intensive evaluation right then and there.

The T-bar makes the Stag very stiff compared to other cars of its time. If the T-bar is missing, the frame is minus an important structural member.

Rust seems to first appear at the base of the B-post where the rear wing joins with the sills. It is a common complaint on poorly-maintained cars. Check also for rust around the wheelarches and on the rear lip of the boot lid. (Courtesy Tony Fox)

The rear shock absorber mounts in the soft top well can rust, and make a costly repair.

The soft top frame needs to be studied to make sure there are no bent frame pieces or frozen joints. A good frame will go up or down very easily and quickly. The header rail is quite often frozen or broken. Replacing the soft top is not an easy or inexpensive DIY project.

Rust and rot on the underside, as well as leaks around the differential and worn joints at the rear driveshafts to the hubs, are a good indication of neglect over the years. (Courtesy Tony Fox)

If the engine does not run, assume the worst – it has suffered from overheating.

(Right) Although a Stag has a vinyl interior, it can be a labour-intensive and costly job to replace, especially if the carpets, hardware, instruments and dash veneer require repair or replacement.

(Left) Avoid any Stag if there is doubt about ownership and commission number, or a total lack of service records.

Buying a Stag at auction is a very risky proposition, regardless of the price, unless the owner is present with full documentation, receipts, restoration and service records. Even then, hearing it run as it goes on the auction block will not allow enough time to make a well informed decision.

Be sure to check the front shock absorber towers under the bonnet – and, likewise, the rear shock absorber mounts in the soft top well.

Check also for rust on the boot lid at the rearmost lip on the underside, as well as the leading edge of the bonnet. (Courtesy Tony Fox)

The engine compartment, other than the shock absorber towers already mentioned, should be fairly solid. Generally, over the years, enough oil will have leaked and circulated throughout the engine compartment to create its own protective coating.

Typical of the vintage, all the wings will rust around the outer lip, but the rear wings can also rust in the lower quarters in front of the wheelarch. These wheelarches and wing edges are prone to rust. Feel the edge to ensure it's the same thickness all the way along. If filler has been used, it will feel built-up in some areas. Squeeze the outside edges as well to ensure that some fresh paint and a thin layer of filler isn't hiding something more sinister. At the same time, feel along the bottoms of the doors and the edge of the boot lid as these areas are susceptible to rust, too.

The front and rear valances or fascias below the bumpers are very susceptible to stone chips and, hence, rust; dings from roadside curbs, and build-up of road dirt.

The best scenario for a comprehensive inspection of the underside is to have the Stag put on a hoist. If covered in undercoating in one area in particular, this could be hiding frame damage or repairs done in the past.

Tap very gently with a screwdriver, or small hammer, on areas that look suspect. Despite the fact that an area may be all rust and rot, the owner won't appreciate you putting a large hole in the frame or floor.

Remember, the frame members are part of the Stag's unibody structure. Areas where the floors meet the outer sills are particularly prone to problems.

Rust in the subframes of a Stag is generally not a problem as these are a thicker gauge steel, although, because they are structural, they still need to be checked carefully.

Although the outriggers may be rusty, these are seldom a failure point as the steel is much heavier gauge than the body. However, check for the rubber body support bushes where the outrigger meets the outer support; these have been known to form a fatigue crack at the welded joint and are not easy to see – don't be afraid of doing a little cleaning off to be certain.

While the outer sills may have appeared rust-free, it is the underside of the sills where possible rot has taken hold. Gently feel and, if suspicious, prod with a screwdriver. If flakey, rust has taken hold and these will have to be replaced. Repair is not simply a matter of a replacement panel, but rather the entire sill and inner castles will require replacement to maintain the overall strength and integrity of the body. Although a common problem, it is an area that will need attention in the near future and the asking price should reflect the extensive work required.

Finally, if the Stag you are considering comes with a hardtop, check the leading edge as this is also an area where rusting occurs.

Exterior trim
Chromework   4 3 2 1

While the Stag is not laden with chrome or stainless trim, replacement is expensive so take stock of which is good and which is bad. The chrome trim around the front grille (horseshoe shapes), tail lights and boot tends to pit. The

stainless rub strips on the rear of the B-pillar are most often deeply scored from the fitting and removal of the hardtop. The chrome latching pads for the hardtop at the rear of the B-pillar are usually pitted, as i s the rear logo plinth on the rear bumper, and the door handle bowls.

The thin trim strip above the rocker panel/sill was fitted during MkI production, although North American cars had the full depth brushed aluminium panel, later adopted for the rest of the world in 1976. There should be blue square British Leyland badges fitted to either side of the front wings.

Check all chrome and stainless trim. The door handle bowls are invariably pitted.

Wipers   4 3 2 1

The Triumph Stag came equipped with two-speed wipers and are unique with its wire frames. Check that the wiper blade is the correct length and in good condition. Before testing, put some water on the windscreen so the wipers don't scratch the glass.

Glass   4 3 2 1

Tinted glass was standard on all North American Stags, and optional on all others.

Windscreens are readily available today at a reasonable cost. The heated rear window of the hardtop is usually in good working order, but still should be tested. All the clips, trim, rubber gaskets and cat's whiskers are readily available. If the windscreen bright trim is missing then this is a problem, as most fitters won't get it back in without removing the glass.

The Triumph Stag came equipped with two-speed wipers, and are unique with wire frames.

There is a distinct difference between North American and European lighting. North American front indicator lights and the sidelights are combined in an amber lens.

There is a distinct difference between North American and European lighting. North American front indicators and the sidelights are combined in an amber lens. European lights have a white and amber combination, with two separate bulbs. North American cars have side marker lights, amber at the front and red at the rear. European cars have no side markers at the rear, and the fronts are indicators.

Rubber

All rubber products, other than quarter light rubbers, are currently available through suppliers.

Convertible and hardtop
The convertible storage hold can leak, and, if the top was not stored correctly, it can be very difficult to erect. Although the owner may have raised or lowered the top, as the potential buyer, you should attempt the procedure. It should fold or erect easily. Before the top is lowered into the hold, the rear section of the bows must be locked in the vertical position using the two latches provided. (Note, though, that only one latch was fitted on the very early models.) If in the past these latches were not locked, it will have caused the rear section to become trapped in the hold. Although instructions were provided in the owner's manual on how to extract it, the bows often became bent. Once the top bows are bent, or out of alignment, it will make raising, fitting and lowering the top very difficult.

While a variety of colours and two types of cloth are available today, the original was black mohair with a lining material. These, too, are still available today from suppliers. Over the years, some cloth tops have been substituted for the less expensive 'double duck' material.

The MkI cars had a soft top with three rear plastic windows which provided good rearward visibility, but were difficult to fold without getting permanent creases in them.

The MkII cars had a larger, single window which was easier to fold without creasing, yet had less rearward visibility. Some MkI cars have since been converted to single window for appearance, and convenience; where the rear quarter

European lights are a white and amber combination with two separate bulbs. North American cars have side marker lights: amber at the front and red at the rear.

MkII cars had a large single window that was easier to fold without creasing, yet had less rearward visibility.

Check that all members of the soft top frame are present and free to move as required when folding. The soft top should not need to be forced when folding. A correctly aligned top will fold in less than a minute.

If the owner has been careful, by unzipping the rear window the top can be folded without creasing the plastic window.

The hardtop is a very useful accessory for owners wishing to drive in the autumn or winter months. It provides a snug interior with good visibility, and also has a heated rear window.

lights tended to get easily scratched and damaged when folded and, in reality, it provided very little in increased visibility.

Many soft top frames have had the header rail joints welded at the outer ends due to breakages. This is not a long-term solution, though, as the joint needs to flex, and, if welded, they will fail again. Check that all members of the soft top frame are present and free to move as required when folding. The soft top should not need to be forced when folding. A correctly aligned top will fold or erect in less than a minute. Check that the rear window is in good shape as replacement requires the top be removed.

Replacing the top is a good day's work for an expert, or a full weekend project for a novice. Be sure to factor in the cost or amount of labour if you contemplate replacing the top, or desire, ultimately, to fit a snazzy colourful new version. Colour coordinated tops do add an extra degree of pizzazz, but not necessarily more value.

The hardtop is a very useful accessory for owners wishing to drive in the autumn or winter months. The hardtop offers a snug interior with good all-round visibility and the added bonus of a heated rear window. Fitting or removing the hardtop is a two person job. Care must be taken when removing to avoid scratches on the B-pillar, the stainless steel cap, and the bodywork. Also, the rear deck often gets scratched or marked if the hardtop is tipped back to the point where a corner makes contact with the panel. If the front upper latches keep coming undone during a road test, the cap on the windscreen header needs to come off and a repair made to the latch pockets.

The colour of the hardtop if it was ordered with the car matches the body colour. If purchased later from a Triumph dealer, it could be painted whatever colour the buyer desired.

Lights

First check to see if all lights are working, then examine the condition of the lenses, the chrome bezels, and the reflective backing plates. Do all the lights and lenses match?

The fuse panel is under the bonnet, attached to the firewall on the right side of the car for LHD cars, and on the left side for RHD Stags. Check that the correct fuses have been fitted. A higher-than-rated fuse can seriously overload the system.

Check that the earth wire from the engine to the body is present. It runs from the front of the engine to the right-hand wing where it is grounded, and then continues on to the negative post on the battery.

Wheels and tyres

Tyres are often new or worn out on cars offered for sale. If new, or only slightly worn, check when the set was fitted; ten-year-old tyres are not what you want on your high performance V8 Stag. For safety reasons all the tyres should match. Steel wheels may be bent or the lip damaged. Check both the inside and the outer. If these wheels require repainting, it means removing the tyre, sandblasting the wheels, re-spraying them silver and then adding the black. This is not a difficult task, but the cost involved due to the amount of labour should be considered. The alloy wheels can also suffer curb damage from parking or from unforgiving automatic car washes. Alloy wheels also suffer from oxidation. The wheels can be sanded and re-sprayed, but, again, there is a considerable cost involved. Most importantly, check that no bolts are broken. The aftermarket alloy wheels are virtually identical to the originals, except for the tyre valve placement. On the originals the tyre valve is at the base of a spoke, while the aftermarket versions place the stem between two spokes.

The chrome on the wire wheels was generally very durable. The apparent rust is often surface only and can be successfully cleaned, but there are limits.

The wire wheels are beautiful, but can be difficult to maintain. Cleaning does take time, but most owners enjoy the task. Yet keeping a wire wheel true and balanced requires specialist knowledge, and the proper equipment is not always available at today's local garages. Wire wheels were standard on Federal cars until mid-1972, when they were replaced by alloy wheels due, in part, to the problems already noted.

The splines for wire wheels tend to wear if the wheel was not put on properly, or tightly fitted. It has also been known for splines to become stuck if they were not greased, causing a problem removing the wheel.

The splines for wire wheels tend to wear if the wheel was not put on properly or tightly fitted. It has also been known for splines to become stuck if they were not greased, causing a problem when trying to remove a wheel.

With the introduction of the MkII Stags, alloy wheels were introduced, standard for North America and optional for the rest of the world. These became standard equipment for all in 1975.

With the growing popularity of alloy wheels, and the difficulties maintaining wire wheels, Triumph began offering alloys as standard on its NA Stags in 1973, and on UK models in 1975.

Any aftermarket wheels, regardless of popularity and expense, tend to reduce the value of a Stag in a collector's eye. Then again, it may be a moot point if driving and performance are the features that have attracted you to owning a Stag.

Tyre size is important on the Stag. Anything above 195–70 section should be used with caution due to possible interference with the car body and suspension.

Wide section tyres are not really suited to the Stag's rear suspension geometry, although many owners fit them for appearance reasons. The car doesn't accommodate wide tyres comfortably as the shoulders of the tyres need to suit the camber changes of the wheel. Look for wear on the tyre and the wheelarches.

Hubs, ball joints, and steering

It is important to make sure there is no play in the lower main pivot ball joint and the track rod end joints, as either will cause wheel shimmy. Make sure the steering rack is not leaking oil, and check the rubber bellows for dampness or being full of oil. Also examine the front and rear wheel bearings for play. Simply rock the wheel top to bottom to find play. Have an assistant hold on the brakes, which should negate any play, while you rock the wheel, then release the brakes and check again for more movement. Of course, the wheel should be jacked-up to get a proper feel for this.

Interior
Upholstery

The seats were always vinyl; although leather was theoretically available, there seems to be no evidence it was ever used. The vinyl used was durable and good wearing material and, therefore, should be quite presentable. Look for the first signs of wear on the backrest piping near the driver's hip position. The squab is padded into shape with a composite foam material to fit the back. The bonding of this material lets go with time – particularly in high temperature climates.

The vinyl used is a durable and hard-wearing material, and should still be quite presentable.

The foam padding crumbles and appears constantly on the carpets. The base squab of the seat does not suffer from this but its support rubber diaphragm often splits, losing support. All these parts are available, or in the case of the backrest an owner can simply carve some foam rubber to shape as an insert. The rear seat is normally in good condition due to limited use.

The UK front seats for MkI Stags had different backrests to the MkII versions. Then again, the US Stags had a unique built-in headrest and large, wide pad. The MkI Stags in the UK had no headrest at all, but instead were fitted with a blanking pad or headroll in its place. A small, adjustable headrest was subsequently adopted for the US and UK on MkII Stags.

The MkI seats differ from MkII items in numerous ways: The backrest tilt latches of the MkII seats, which allow access to the rear compartment, were positioned lower down to make them more accessible. The MkII seats were offered with headrests for safety reasons. (Note, the North American MkI Stags were always equipped with headrests.)

On all Stags, the backrest of the front seats could be adjusted for rake, and the lower cushions could be tilted and the seat itself adjusted fore and aft.

Due to changing safety regulations, there were three different styles of seatbelt fitted during production; the third type was unique to 1977.

Look for worn webbing on the seatbelts of high mileage cars. Replacing the seatbelts is, surprisingly, an expensive proposition due to safety regulations. Still, to replace the belts is a fairly straightforward task.

Later Stags, from 1976 onward, had a plastic hook near the top of the B-pillar that enabled the seatbelt buckle to be stored out of the way when not in use. Often, owners have added these to early Stags.

New door panels are available in either complete units or, simply, as new backing card.

Door trim and handles

The interior door panels are often warped, and occasionally retained by screws instead of the correct push-in clips. New door panels are available; in either complete units or, simply, a new backing card. Overall, the interior trim was a good quality vinyl, but can still suffer from cuts, wear, and broken piping. There were two types of door latches; MkIIs had plastic surrounds and different strikers, whereas the MkI Stag's were all metal.

Mats and carpets

The MkI Stag was fitted with wool pile carpet, while the MkII was downgraded to tufted nylon. Usually the carpets were colour coordinated with body colours, although black was the most common.

Replacing the carpets is costly and time-consuming, but completely achievable by the home mechanic.

Other shades included light and dark brown, blue and red. The correct carpet sets should have the 'Triumph' name in the heel pads. Replacing the carpets is costly and time consuming, but completely achievable by the home mechanic.

A 16in diameter steering wheel was fitted on the MkI model, while a smaller, 14½in wheel was standard on MkII Stags, as shown here.

Steering wheel and column

The column is adjustable up and down and can telescope. Two different sizes of steering wheel were fitted; a 16in diameter on MkI models, and a 14½in wheel on MkII Stags. Many owners prefer the smaller wheel for better feel and more knee room. These are directly interchangeable.

Dashboard, instruments and controls

A small rubber mat was placed in the top of the dash catch-all. This is usually missing.

The instruments on the MkI cars had black bezels and the needles pointed downward ...

Minor changes were made to the fascia which differentiate a MkI from a MkII Stag. Rather than a map light in the glovebox lid, MkII Stags featured a dash light above the central console. It is quite common for the finish of the veneer on the dash to be cracked. This can be refinished, though, as the actual wood veneer is most often in good shape.

The instruments on MkI Stags had black bezels and the needles pointed downward, whereas the MkII Stag featured chrome bezels and the needles pointed upward. The MkII models also had green backlighting to the instruments. Most often, the clock is not functional on any Stag.

Check that the heater on/off control actually regulates the heat output, as the valve on the heater can seize.

... whereas, the MkII Stag featured chrome bezels and the needles pointed upward, together with green backlighting for a more modern appearance.

Very little changed in the way of controls during production, other than the wipers, which had an intermittent feature added to the MkII cars. The overdrive switch was always located in the gearstick knob. A left footrest was added in the MkII Stags and, for 1977 only, a different handbrake cover was used.

Keys

There were two Stag keys. The large key was used for the ignition, door locks, and the fuel filler security cover. The small key was used for the glovebox and the boot lock.

Mechanicals
Engine

The most notorious of Stag problems was overheating. Unfortunately, this is its legacy. Most of the Stags still on the road today should have all of that behind them, but don't take the seller's word on this. Drive the car for twenty minutes to get it good and hot, and then let it idle for another twenty minutes. The temperature gauge will tell you immediately if the engine has problems. As noted in chapter 7, if the indicated temperature crosses the midway mark, heading for the 'hot' zone, it is time to walk away or get some serious price adjustments made as you could be faced with some significant repairs. If you are uncomfortable assessing this situation, bring along an expert for this important issue.

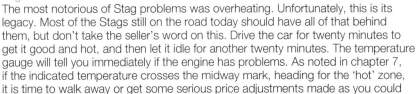

The fairly reliable Stromberg carburettors often suffer from owners who feel they must tinker with them. Normally, these carbs give trouble-free running without interference.

It has been reported that three-quarters of all the Stags sent to the US suffered from overheating problems.

Also, look carefully around the cylinder heads to see if any joints or core plugs have been covered up with an external sealer.

Carburettors and manifold

The Stromberg carburettors are fairly reliable and trouble free. Many owners have fitted alternative modern carburettors to provide better performance for the same fuel economy.

There was a Stag recall in 1971-72 regarding the possibility of the throttle jamming wide open.

Transmissions

Most Stags are automatics and, thus, a 4-speed sells for a premium. Many automatic transmission Stags have been converted to 4-speeds using a Jaguar ZF unit. This is a fairly straightforward conversion that will cost in the region of ●x2000. It adds a little to the value, transforms the Stag into a quieter, more relaxed touring car with lower rpm and improved fuel consumption.

Some more modern carbs, such as a Holley, provide better performance for the same fuel economy.

Cooling system

While MkI systems had the pressure cap on the right side of the radiator, MkII Stags had a sealed radiator with the pressure cap on the expansion bottle. Check the cold radiator carefully for leaks or dissolving fins before removing the cap. Is there anti-freeze in the system? Water in a radiator can cause internal corrosion. If the Stag is running, check that the radiator gets fairly evenly hot across both tanks. If not, it could indicate a blocked system. The MkII Stags had a higher compression engine and a different air intake system. A thermostatically-controlled air intake was introduced in 1972, just at the end of MkI production.

Steering

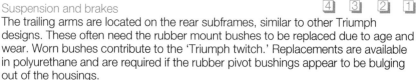

This is not usually a problem area, but check for leaks from the power assisted rack. Leaks usually mean a rebuild, although there are power steering sealing fluids that add many more miles to the rack before it needs attention. Carefully inspect the bellows on each end to make sure these are not split. The power steering has a light feel that's sensitive on the road. There was a recall surrounding a problem with the upper U-joint in the steering column.

During the road test the steering should have a light, smooth action. Any 'notchy' feeling is not a good sign and could mean a rebuild.

Suspension and brakes

The trailing arms are located on the rear subframes, similar to other Triumph designs. These often need the rubber mount bushes to be replaced due to age and wear. Worn bushes contribute to the 'Triumph twitch.' Replacements are available in polyurethane and are required if the rubber pivot bushings appear to be bulging out of the housings.

Check for rusty brake lines and hoses that look aged. Older hoses tend to swell internally, allowing fluid under pressure to the brakes but restricting the return. This causes the brakes to stay on, with subsequent overheating and wear, and may account for poor braking performance. A long pedal travel could mean worn brakes, or the rear brake self-adjusting mechanism isn't working.

Wiring, battery and charging

The battery tray is always prone to rust as water tends to get trapped between the battery and the metal framework. Check, also, that the battery clamp is securely in place and not missing. Unfortunately, it is not easy to remove the battery to check this due to the position of the power steering pump. It is not necessary to disconnect the pump, but rather just move it aside to allow clearance for the battery to be removed.

Fuel tank and lines

Check the seams carefully for corrosion. If the Stag hasn't moved for a while, or has its original fuel tank, ask if the tank has ever been re-lined or blown-out. Rust and sludge build-up at the bottom of the fuel tank of every old car, and this is one of the main sources of a car stalling or not running smoothly. An early 1970s Stag recall concerned the splitting of the fuel filler hose.

Oil leaks

Minor oil leaks are common with most old cars, even if restored to concours condition. Thus, these minor leaks are generally considered more of a nuisance than a sign of a serious problem. The Stag is certainly no exception. Look for leaks on the engine, oil pump housing, valve covers, head gaskets in the 'V' of the block, and front and rear crankshaft seals.

The rear differential is prone to leaks around the rear cover, side output shaft seals and the

Carefully check the fuel tank seams for corrosion, as well as the fuel lines for rust, especially at joins.
(Courtesy Tony Fox)

The Stag V8 engine should be checked over carefully, before and after starting, for oil leaks. Common areas for oil leaks include: around the valve covers; the oil pump housing; the head gaskets, and on the front and rear crankshaft seats.

front pinion seal. A blocked breather at the top right rear could cause this. Automatic transmissions are notorious for leaking, particularly when parked for a couple of weeks. The oil can leak onto the exhaust, causing a smell when the exhaust is hot.

Exhaust

The original design from Triumph is a dual pipe system exiting on the left rear side of the car. Make sure it has this design, which provides a distinct character to the Stag. A standard conversion, today, is to a stainless steel system for durability.

The Triumph Stag was always fitted with this type of dual exhaust system. The MkI Stag exhaust tailpipes were 'large bore' 2½in (6.25cm), while the MkII, in 1973, went to the 'small bore' 2in (5cm) size.

Test drive (not less than 15 minutes)

The most important thing to establish with a Stag is a successful test run. You should find the car comfortable and well handling with good power.

You may enjoy the drive, but don't let that distract you. Does the engine smoke? Are there any unusual noises, clunks or rattles? Does this Stag steer and stop straight? Are the brakes hot after a short drive? If the temperature gauge reads higher than normal ask the owner about overheating.

During your road test it is better to have the top up so you can hear any noises more easily – the wind can hide a multitude of noises.

Driving a Stag with the manual transmission, listen for noisy bearings at idle and in the intermediate gears. If you can beat the synchromesh, particularly on second and third gears, then there is wear.

Try all the gears to make sure they don't disengage on the overrun. If this happens, an overhaul is required. The shift should be positive and precise, and the clutch should take up smoothly, both cold and hot, with no jerkiness. The overdrive should engage sharply in and out of gear at driving speeds of 60-70mph. Any delay in engagement means wear and possible repairs.

Generally, the Borg Warner automatic transmissions are tough units. A worn automatic transmission can be characterised by harsh downshifting into first when coming to a stop. Check each gear for crisp shifting, both up and down the range. Does the kick-down feature work?

You will find that engaging first or reverse from a standstill often produces quite a clunk from the driveline. This can be caused by the engine idle being set higher than 800rpm. Other factors can influence transmission performance: looseness in the driveline components, or wear in the propshaft joints, rear axle shaft joints and differential.

While on the road, listen carefully for a whine from the rear axle. Worn out rear ends can develop a whine, either when on load or on the overrun.

The driveshaft splines going from the differential to the hubs have the common characteristic of sticking, causing the famous 'Triumph twitch' which you will feel while driving. This is caused when the telescoping splines become dry or worn, and stick during cornering as the shaft needs to change length. The 'letting go' process causes the twitch. It can normally be resolved by applying fresh anti-seize grease to the splines.

It is difficult to assess wear on the outer

During your road test it is better to have the top up, so you can more easily hear any noises, as the wind can hide a multitude of sounds.

Generally, the Borg Warner transmissions are tough units, yet not without some concerns.

universal joints, but it can be done with some effort. If worn, the whole shaft needs to come out. Early models were fitted with universal joints that had staked joints instead of the more common circlip retainers. These are not easy to change, and it is simpler to purchase a replacement shaft complete with wheel hub. Regardless of model, this is an expensive repair.

Of course, worn or soft rear suspension rubber mounts can exaggerate this 'twitch,' too.

Check that the brakes are not getting hot after your test drive. It is not uncommon for old brake hoses to become swollen and closed up on the inside. This will allow fluid to the brakes under pressure from the master cylinder, but not to return under brake return spring pressure. This, of course, can cause overheating of either the front or rear brakes, depending which hose is at fault. A front hose closure will generally cause the car to pull to one side.

Stag optional equipment
Wire wheels and aluminium wheels
Four-speed transmission with overdrive
Hardtop
AC (up until 1976)
Automatic transmission
Tinted glass
Headrests on MkII models

Thirty-three original body colours were offered during the production life of the Triumph Stag.

Modifications
With today's 'driving classics' originality is not stressed, as many owners prefer a Stag that is more convenient and pleasant, safer, performs better and is able to keep up with modern traffic. The following is a list of fairly common Stag upgrades:

Electric cooling fan with temperature control
Holley, Edelbrock or Weber carburettor or fuel injection conversion
Suspension changes, including improved shock absorbers
Four piston front calipers, rear disc brakes and larger brake servo
4-speed with OD, ZF Automatic transmission
Engine transplants, such as the Rover 3.5 V8, Ford V6 or GM V6.
Reduction high torque starter motors
Exhaust headers
Upgraded alternator
Halogen, Xenon or high intensity lighting
Non-stick telescoping design rear driveshaft
Aftermarket aluminium wheels, such as Minilites, Wolfrace or Panasports
Upgraded walnut veneer dash
MkII steering wheel on MkI models
Aftermarket windbreakers with vinyl cover over the rear seat
Coloured soft tops, in either mohair or double duck material
Electronic ignition
Polyurethane suspension bushings
Rear trailing arm tie bars
Electric water pump
Stainless steel exhaust system
Seatbelt hooks
Leather seating kits
Electronic fuel pump
Oil pressure gauge fitted in place of the clock
Upgraded AC pump
Front spoiler
Wire wheel retainers to switch to a 2- or 3-ear design
BMW differential
High performance brake pads
Heavy-duty timing chains
Suspension lowering kit
Spin-on oil filter
Engine oil cooler
Armoured brake hoses
Redundant bonnet release cable

Evaluation procedure

Add up the total points. Score: **116 = excellent, possibly concours;
87 = good; 58 = average; 29 = poor**. Cars scoring over 81 should be
completely useable and require the minimum of repair, although continued
maintenance and care will be required to keep them in condition. Cars scoring
between 29-56 will require serious restoration (at much the same cost). Cars scoring
between 60-80 will require very carefull assessment of necessary repair/restoration
costs in order to reach a realistic value.

10 Auctions
– sold! Another way to buy your dream

Auction pros & cons
Pros: Prices will usually be lower than those of dealers or private sellers and you might grab a real bargain on the day. Auctioneers have usually established clear title with the seller. At the venue you can usually examine documentation relating to the vehicle.

Cons: You have to rely on a sketchy catalogue description of condition and history. The opportunity to inspect is limited and you cannot take the Stag on a performance test drive. Vehicles could well be a little below par and are likely to require some work. It's easy to overbid. There will usually be a buyer's premium to pay in addition to the auction hammer price.

Which auction?
Auctions by established auctioneers are advertised in car magazines and on the auction houses' websites. A catalogue, or a simple printed list of the lots for auctions might be available only a day or two ahead, though often lots are listed and pictured on auctioneers' websites much earlier. Contact the auction company to ask if previous auction selling prices are available as this is useful information (details of past sales are often available on websites).

Catalogue, entry fee and payment details
When you purchase the catalogue of the vehicles in the auction, it often acts as a ticket allowing two people to attend the viewing days and the auction. Catalogue details tend to be comparatively brief, but will include information such as 'one owner from new, low mileage, full service history,' etc. It will also usually show a guide price to give you some idea of what to expect to pay and will tell you what is charged as a 'buyer's premium.' The catalogue will also contain details of acceptable forms of payment. At the fall of the hammer an immediate deposit is usually required, the balance payable within 24 hours. If the plan is to pay by cash there may be a cash limit. Some auctions will accept payment by debit card. Sometimes credit or charge cards are acceptable, but will often incur an extra charge. A bank draft or bank transfer will have to be arranged in advance with your own bank as well as with the auction house. No vehicle will be released before **all** payments are cleared. If delays occur in payment transfers then storage costs can accrue.

Buyer's premium
A buyer's premium will be added to the hammer price; **don't** forget this in your calculations. It is not usual for there to be a further state tax or local tax on the purchase price and/or on the buyer's premium.

Viewing
In some instances, it's possible to view on the day, or days before, as well as in the hours prior to the auction. There are auction officials available who are willing to help out by opening engine and luggage compartments and to allow you to inspect the interior. While the officials may start the engine for you, a test drive is out of the

question. Crawling under and around the Stag as much as you want is permitted, but you can't suggest that the vehicle you are interested in be jacked up, or attempt to do the job yourself. You can also ask to see any documentation available.

Bidding
Before you take part in the auction, **decide your maximum bid – and stick to it!**

It may take a while for the auctioneer to reach the lot you are interested in, so use that time to observe how other bidders behave. When it's the turn of your vehicle, attract the auctioneer's attention and make an early bid. The auctioneer will then look to you for a reaction every time another bid is made, usually the bids will be in fixed increments until the bidding slows, when smaller increments will often be accepted before the hammer falls. If you want to withdraw from the bidding, make sure the auctioneer understands your intentions – a vigorous shake of the head when he or she looks to you for the next bid should do the trick!

Assuming that you are the successful bidder the auctioneer will note your card or paddle number and, from that moment on, you will be responsible for the vehicle.

If the Stag is unsold, either because it failed to reach the reserve or because there was little interest, it may be possible to negotiate with the owner, via the auctioneers, after the sale is over.

Successful bid
There are two more items to think about: how to get the Stag home, and insurance. If you can't drive the vehicle, your own or a hired trailer is one way. Another is to have the vehicle shipped using the facilities of a local company. The auction house will also have details of companies specialising in the transfer of all types of vehicle.

Insurance for immediate cover can usually be purchased on site, but it may be more cost-effective to make arrangements with your own insurance company in advance, and then call to confirm the full details. (Don't forget classic vehicle insurance where appropriate.)

eBay & other online auctions
Buying this way could land you a Stag at a bargain price, though you'd be foolhardy to bid without examining the car first, something most vendors encourage. A useful feature of eBay is that the geographical location of the vehicle is shown, so you can narrow your choices to those within a realistic radius of home. Be prepared to be outbid in the last few moments of the auction. Remember, your bid is binding and that it will be very, very difficult to get restitution in the case of a crooked vendor fleecing you – caveat emptor!

Be aware that some vehicles offered for sale in online auctions are 'ghost' vehicles. **Don't** part with **any** cash without being sure that the Stag does actually exist and is as described (usually pre-bidding inspection is possible).

Auctioneers
Barrett-Jackson www.barrett-jackson.com **Bonhams** www.bonhams.com
British Car Auctions BCA) www.bca-europe.com/www.british-car- auctions.co.uk
Christies www.christies.com **Coys** www.coys.co.uk
eBay www.ebay.com/www.ebay.co.uk **H&H** www.handh.co.uk
RM Sotheby's www.rmsothebys.com **Shannons** www.shannons.com.au
Silver www.silverauctions.com

11 Paperwork

– correct documentation is essential!

The paper trail

Classic, collector and prestige cars usually come with a large portfolio of paperwork accumulated and passed on by a succession of proud owners. This documentation represents the real history of the Stag, and from it can be deduced the level of care the vehicle has received, how much it's been used, which specialists have worked on it, and the dates of major repairs and restorations. All of this information will be priceless to you as the new owner, so be very wary of Stags with little paperwork to support their claimed history.

Registration documents

All countries/states have some form of registration for private vehicles, whether it's like the American 'pink slip' system or the British 'log book' system.

It is essential to check that the registration document is genuine, that it relates to the Stag in question, and that all the vehicle's details are correctly recorded, including chassis/VIN and engine numbers (if these are shown). If you are buying from the previous owner, his or her name and address will be recorded in the document: this will not be the case if you are buying from a dealer.

In the UK, the current (Euro-aligned) registration document is named 'V5C,' and is printed in coloured sections of blue, green and pink. The blue section relates to the vehicle's specification, the green section has details of the new owner, and the pink section is sent to the DVLA in the UK when the vehicle is sold. A small section in yellow deals with selling the car within the motor trade.

In the UK the DVLA will provide details of earlier keepers of the vehicle upon payment of a small fee, and much can be learned in this way.

If the Stag has a foreign registration there may be expensive and time-consuming formalities to complete. Do you really want the hassle?

Roadworthiness certificate

Most country/state administrations require that vehicles are regularly tested to prove that they are safe to use on the public highway and do not produce excessive emissions. In the UK that test (the 'MoT') is carried out at approved testing stations, for a fee. In the USA the requirement varies, but most states insist on an emissions test every two years as a minimum, while the police are charged with pulling over unsafe-looking vehicles.

In the UK, the test is required on an annual basis once a vehicle becomes three years old. Of particular relevance for older cars is that the certificate issued includes the mileage reading recorded at the test date and, therefore, becomes an independent record of that vehicle's history. Ask the seller if previous certificates are available. Without an MoT the vehicle should be hauled by trailer to its new home, unless you insist that a valid MoT is part of the deal (not such a bad idea this, as at least you will know the Stag was roadworthy on the day it was tested and you don't need to wait for the old certificate to expire before having the test done).

Road licence

The administration of every country/state charges some kind of tax for the use of its road system, the actual form of the 'road licence,' and how it is displayed, varying enormously country-to-country and state-to-state.

Whatever the form of the road licence, it must relate to the vehicle carrying it and must be present and valid if the vehicle is to be driven on the public highway legally. The value of the licence will depend on what duration it will be valid for.

Changed legislation in the UK means that the seller of a car must surrender any existing road fund licence, and it is the responsibility of the new owner to re-tax the vehicle at the time of purchase and before the car can be driven on the road. It's therefore vital to see the Vehicle Registration Certificate (V5C) at the time of purchase, and to have access to the New Keeper Supplement (V5C/2), allowing the buyer to obtain road tax immediately. If the car is untaxed because it has not been used for a period of time, the owner has to inform the licensing authorities, otherwise the vehicle's date-related registration number will be lost and there will be a painful amount of paperwork to get it re-registered.

Certificates of authenticity

For many makes of collectable car it is possible to get a certificate proving the age and authenticity (e.g. engine and chassis numbers, paint colour and trim) of a particular vehicle. These are sometimes called 'Heritage Certificates' and if the Stag

The smooth V8 engine and Michelotti styling are the essential elements of the Stag's unique character.

comes with one of these it is a definite bonus. If you want to obtain one, the relevant owners' club is the best starting point.

If the car has been used in European classic car rallies it may have a FIVA (Fédération Internationale des Véhicules Anciens) certificate. The so-called 'FIVA Passport,' or 'FIVA Vehicle Identity Card,' enables organisers and participants to recognise whether or not a particular vehicle is suitable for individual events. If you want to obtain such a certificate go to www.fbhvc.co.uk or www.fiva.org, there will be similar organisations in other countries too.

Valuation certificate

Hopefully, the vendor will have a recent valuation certificate, or letter signed by a recognised expert stating how much he, or she, believes the particular Stag to be worth (such documents, together with photos, are usually needed to get 'agreed value' insurance). Generally, such documents should act only as confirmation of your own assessment of the Stag, rather than a guarantee of value, as the expert has probably not seen the car in the flesh. The easiest way to find out how to obtain a formal valuation is to contact the owners' club.

Service history

Often these cars will have been serviced at home by enthusiastic (and hopefully capable) owners for a good number of years. Nevertheless, try to obtain as much service history and other paperwork pertaining to the car as you can. Naturally, dealer stamps, or specialist garage receipts score most points in the value stakes. However, anything helps in the great authenticity game, items like the original bill of sale, handbook, parts invoices and repair bills, adding to the story and the character of the Stag. Even a brochure correct to the year of the car's manufacture is a useful document and something that you could well have to search hard to locate in future years. If the seller claims that the Stag has been restored, then expect receipts and other evidence from a specialist restorer.

If the seller claims to have carried out regular servicing, ask what work was completed, when, and seek some evidence of it being carried out. Your assessment of the car's overall condition should tell you whether the seller's claims are genuine.

Restoration photographs

If the seller tells you that the Stag has been restored, then expect to be shown a series of photographs taken while the restoration was under way. Pictures taken at various stages, and from various angles, should help you gauge the thoroughness of the work. If you buy the Stag, ask if you can have all the photographs because they form an important part of the vehicle's history. It's surprising how many sellers are happy to part with their car and accept your cash, but want to hang on to their photographs! In the latter event, you may be able to persuade the vendor to get a set of copies made.

Previous ownership records

Due to the introduction of important new legislation on data protection, it is no longer possible to acquire, from the British DVLA, a list of previous owners of a car you own, or are intending to purchase. This scenario will also apply to dealerships and other specialists, from who you may wish to make contact and acquire information on previous ownership and work carried out.

12 What's it worth to you?
– let your head rule your heart!

Condition

If the Stag you've been looking at is really bad, then you've probably not bothered to use the marking system in chapter 9 – 60 minute evaluation. You may not have even got as far as using that chapter at all!

If you did use the marking system in chapter 9, you'll know whether the car is in Excellent (maybe concours), Good, Average or Poor condition or, perhaps, somewhere in-between these categories.

Many classic/collector car magazines run a regular price guide. If you haven't bought the latest editions, do so now and compare their suggested values for the model you are thinking of buying – also look at the auction prices they're reporting. Values have been fairly stable for a while, but some models will always be more sought after than others. Trends can change, too. The values published in the magazines tend to vary from one magazine to another, as do their scales of condition, so read carefully the guidance notes they provide. Bear in mind that a car that is truly a recent show winner could be worth more than the highest scale published. Assuming that the Stag you have in mind is not in show/concours condition, relate the level of condition that you judge the car to be in with the appropriate guide price. How does the figure compare with the asking price? Before you start haggling with the seller, consider what effect any variation from standard specification might have on the car's value.

If you are buying from a dealer, remember there will be a dealer's premium on the price.

Desirable options/extras

For Stag owners there are two key options that directly affect the buying price, though they are often of no interest to many potential owners.

Firstly, the snug fitting, well appointed hardtop is most often desirable to those who really prefer touring in GT style and enjoying air conditioned comfort. With the blazing sun and golden tans no longer being the attraction they were in the past, many prefer a 'cooler' drive. For those enthusiasts a hardtop is essential, yet for others even putting up the cloth top in a light rain spoils the enjoyment of the ride. For lovers of open-air motoring a hardtop is just another bulky item for them to store in their garage. Then again, a large number of owners prefer to store their Stag in bad weather knowing they have the security of the hardtop to thwart crooks and creatures. The hardtop is heavy (approximately 150lb or 68kg) and is normally painted in the same colour as the body, but, there was the option for the hardtop to be delivered in primer so that it could be painted whatever shade the owner desired. A two-tone Stag is a rare sight, but nonetheless could be original.

Secondly, the chrome wire wheels. For some, wire wheels are a major defining point with British sports models and enhance the Stag's appearance considerably. Others see wire wheels as difficult to clean, keep balanced and well maintained. Wire wheels were never an option in Britain or Europe; being available only on Federal Stags until the end of 1972. Today, wire wheels are a familiar sight on both sides of the Atlantic. Standard steel wheels with Rostyle trims were available right from the start of production. The later MkII optional 5-spoke wheels eventually becoming standard. Be aware that reproduction alloy wheels, when fitted, differ in the position of the valve stem (between the spokes), and feature domed, rather than concave, wheel nuts.

British Leyland offered a host of optional equipment for its Specialist Division cars. These included mirrors, lamps, floor mats, mud guards, towing equipment, badge bars, etc. which means owners could easily personalise their Stag.

The list of available exterior paint colours changed each year, with only white being available unchanged from 1971 to 1977. There were always various shades of yellows, blues, greens and reds. Sienna Brown is the least desirable colour, and there was never a silver or grey.

The vinyl interior was available in various colours depending on the year. Black was always offered, as were browns, including Saddle Tan and Chestnut Brown. Rarest is Inca Red, which was offered only in 1971. Shadow Blue vinyl could be ordered from 1971 into 1975.

Striking a deal

Negotiate on the basis of your condition assessment, mileage, and fault rectification cost. Also take into account the car's specification. Be realistic about the value, but don't be completely intractable: a small compromise on the part of the vendor or buyer will often facilitate a deal at little real cost.

13 Do you really want to restore?

– it'll take longer and cost more than you think

Restoring a Stag is very feasible today as the parts supply situation is extremely good. Just about any part you might want is available, either new or used. However, from a practical point of view it may not be economically feasible. Buy the best Stag you can afford as it may be less expensive in the long run.

Before buying such a project ask yourself, or get advice on, whether you can afford (both financially and time wise) to go this route. If, however, you have the abilities and the desire to rebuild a Stag, there is plenty of assistance and expertise available.

Buying a Stag you can drive while restoring it adds considerable enjoyment to a long-term project.

The Stag Owners' club in the UK created the Tooling Fund (SOCTFL) several years ago to ensure that body panels could be sourced for a rebuild. There are also a number of very good self-help avenues available if you are internet savvy. The Stag Digest is a chat group for enthusiasts, and provides restoration information and guidance when needed. An alternative is the Stag Forum; a question and answer facility sponsored by dedicated Stag enthusiasts. Overall, there is a close-knit family of dedicated Stag enthusiasts around the world with the expertise and knowledge. Knowledge of newer production methods and technology continues to increase, to the benefit of all Stag owners.

Stags often appear after being in storage for years, chiefly due to engine problems. These Stags never received the required 'fixes' that became available over the years. As a result, most require a total engine rebuild, which is costly, whether performed by the owner or professionally.

Keep in mind, though, that the rebuild shops have developed the necessary expertise to deal with the Stag's inherent problems.

Don't underestimate the amount of work involved. It is always more than you think, even with all this advice being available. Restoration always ends up with surprises because the condition of the car is invariably worse than you ever imagined.

If you purchase a project car, prepare and plan the restoration very carefully. Consider if you

Don't underestimate the amount of work involved!

Triumph Stags are increasing in value and interest, but, as is the case with many cars, the cost of a full concours restoration at a professional shop will soon exceed its market value.

have the space required for a dismantled Stag, as well as the ability to work during the colder months of the year?

Are you prepared, and do you have the ability, to complete all the bodywork and re-paint? A poor amateur restoration, despite the money invested, has less market value than a clean, unrestored, unmolested original. At the same time, an abandoned project by an enthusiast has little resale value. A partially finished car is difficult to assess and could be missing parts that will cost the potential buyer more money.

A rolling restoration you can drive and enjoy is perhaps a far better solution than a non-runner. Remember, restoration is labour intensive and the cost of a professional restoration will easily exceed a Stag's market value. Keep in mind, even a Stag requiring mild interior, chrome, engine, mechanical, body and paint work can outstrip the price of a very good, turn-key driver you could enjoy immediately.

Beyond having the money, skill and ambition to restore a Stag, it requires a suitable place to work. To do a restoration you need space, an environment conducive to working in, all the tools, electricity, and good lighting.

14 Paint problems
– a bad complexion, including dimples, pimples and bubbles

Paint faults generally occur due to lack of protection/maintenance, or to poor preparation prior to a respray or touch-up. Some of the following conditions may be present in the car you're looking at:

Orange peel
This appears as an uneven paint surface, similar to the appearance of the skin of an orange. The fault is caused by the failure of atomised paint droplets to flow into each other when they hit the surface. It's sometimes possible to rub out the effect with proprietary paint cutting/rubbing compound or very fine grades of abrasive paper. A respray may be necessary in severe cases. Consult a bodywork repairer/paint shop for advice on the particular vehicle.

Fading paint is normally obvious. Some faded paint can be restored through the use of commercially developed rubbing compounds.

Cracking
Severe cases are likely to have been caused by too heavy an application of paint (or filler beneath the paint). Also, insufficient stirring of the paint before application can lead to the components being improperly mixed, and cracking can result. Incompatibility with the paint already on the panel can have a similar effect. To rectify, it is necessary to rub down to a smooth, sound finish before re-spraying the problem area.

Cracking and blistering paint due to poor storage can occur in unexpected areas, such as on the rear cowl and boot lid.

Crazing
Sometimes the paint takes on a crazed, rather than a cracked, appearance when the problems mentioned under 'Cracking' are present. This problem can also be caused by a reaction between the underlying surface and the paint. Paint removal and re-spraying the problem area is usually the only solution.

Blistering
Almost always caused by corrosion of the metal beneath the paint. Usually perforation will be found in the metal and the damage will usually be worse than that suggested by the area of blistering. The metal will have to be repaired before repainting.

Blistering paint can denote corrosion underneath.

Micro blistering

Usually the result of an economy re-spray where inadequate heating has allowed moisture to settle on the vehicle before spraying. Consult a paint specialist, but usually damaged paint will have to be removed before partial or full re-spraying. Can also be caused by vehicle covers that don't 'breathe.'

Fading

Some colours, especially reds, are prone to fading if subjected to strong sunlight for long periods without the benefit of polish protection. Sometimes proprietary paint restorers and/or paint cutting/rubbing compounds will retrieve the situation. Often a re-spray is the only real solution.

Red and maroon shades are the most susceptible to fading.

Peeling

Often a problem with metallic paintwork when the sealing lacquer becomes damaged and begins to peel off. Poorly applied paint may also peel. The remedy is to strip and start again!

Dimples

Dimples in the paintwork are caused by the residue of polish (particularly silicone types) not being removed properly before re-spraying. Paint removal and repainting is the only solution.

Minor dents can often be rectified, as long as the paint finish has not been damaged.

Dents

Small dents are usually easily cured by the 'Dentmaster,' or equivalent process, that sucks or pushes out the dent (as long as the paint surface is still intact). Companies offering dent removal services usually come to your home – consult your telephone directory.

Although nice, metallic paint has its own set of problems as it ages.

15 Problems due to lack of use
– just like their owners, Stags need exercise!

Seized components
Pistons in calipers and slave and master cylinders can rust and seize. The clutch may seize if the plate becomes stuck to the flywheel because of corrosion. Handbrakes (parking brakes) can seize if the cables and linkages rust. Under the bonnet, valves may stick in cylinder heads and pistons can seize in the bores due to corrosion. Turn over the engine by hand to see if it has 360 degrees of rotation. Stromberg carburettor pistons stick, but can easily be freed.

Seized components, deteriorated rubber fittings, rust and leaks are all signs of an underused, or long time storage, Stag.

Fluids
Old, acidic, oil can corrode bearings. If parked with a blown cylinder head gasket, expect bore damage from anti-freeze. Uninhibited coolant can corrode internal waterways. Lack of anti-freeze can cause core plugs to be pushed out, even cracks in the block or head. Silt settling and solidifying can cause overheating. Coolant loses protective properties after a few years.

Old brake fluid can cause brake failure when the water turns to vapour near hot braking components. The Borg Warner automatic transmission invariably loses fluid if parked for long periods.

Tyre problems
Tyres that have had the weight of the car on them in a single position for some time will develop flat spots, resulting in some (usually temporary) vibration. The tyre walls may have cracks or (blister-type) bulges, meaning new tyres are needed.

Shock absorbers (dampers)
With lack of use, dampers will lose their elasticity or even seize. Creaking, groaning and stiff suspension are signs of this problem.

Rubber and plastic
Radiator hoses may have perished and split, possibly resulting in the loss of all coolant. Window and door seals can harden and leak. Gaitors/boots can crack. Wiper blades will harden.

Electrics
The battery will be of little use if it has not been charged for many months. Earthing/grounding problems are common on fuel pump, alternator, etc., due to corroded connections. Old bullet- and spade-type electrical connectors commonly rust/corrode and will need disconnecting, cleaning and protection (i.e. Vaseline). Spark plug electrodes will often have corroded in an unused engine. Wiring insulation can harden and fail, or be chewed by rodents.

Convertible top

Ragtops that have been folded for a considerable time can have severe window creases, and the frames can seize.

Rotting exhaust system

Exhaust gas contains a high water content so exhaust systems corrode very quickly from the inside when the car is not used.

The interior of a well-used or stored car can deteriorate surprisingly quickly.

– key people, organisations and companies in the Stag world

Clubs

Belgian Stag Owners' Club
Gilbert Ronge, Socialstraat 17, B-3600
Genk, Belgium

British Saloon Car Club of Canada
Roger Tipple, 1404 Baldwin Ave,
Burlington, ON L7S 1K3, Canada

German Stag Owners' Club
Christian Schluter, Heimstattenweg 22,
32052 Herford, Germany

Netherlands Stag Owners' Club
Pieter Berkhout, Julianaweg 16, NL
2243 HT Wassenaar, Netherlands

Stag Owners' Club, UK (SOC)
Derek Athey, The Old Rectory, Aslacton,
Norfolk, NR15 2JN

Stag Owners' Club of Australia
PO Box 501, Fullarton SA 5063,
Australia

Stag Owners' Club of New Zealand
Ian Skene, PO Box 93, West Park
Village, West Harbour, Waitakere 0661,
Auckland, New Zealand

Swiss Stag Owners' Club
Daniel Moser, Gyrisbergstr 122, 3400
Burgdorf, Switzerland

Toronto Triumph Club
Larry Llewellyn, PO Box 39, Don Mills,
ON. M3C 2R6, Canada

Triumph Stag Club Austria
Roy P Carvana, PO Box 35, 2823 Pitten,
Austria

Triumph Stag Club USA (TSC USA)
Michael Coffey, 401 Brighton Drive,
Clarks Green, PA 18411 USA

United Kingdom

The Stag Owners' Club (SOC) was formed in the mid-1970s by Tony Hart, and
has since become a 5000 strong member club with chapters across the UK. Hart
also formed Hart Racing Services (HRS), which provided an approach to shoring
up the Stag's bad reputation in the 1970s. He successfully raced a Stag with the
standard 3-litre engine, giving it some credibility for reliability and performance. He
also became the person to go to for Stag repairs and rebuilds in the UK, and from
around the world.

North America

The Stag Club USA (SCUSA) was formed in the mid-1990s by Michael Coffey
in Pennsylvania. The same principles adopted by Tony Hart were employed to
form this club in order to support and preserve the Stag in NA. It has grown to
around 250 members in the USA and Canada. His dedication to the marque has
undoubtedly been a big factor in its resurgence in North America, after a disastrous
reputation in the 1970s. There were only 2871 Stags sold in the USA between
1971 to 1973. Canada never did receive the Stag, as British Leyland Canada made
the business decision not to import them; according to interviews with ex-BLMC
executives in Canada.

Stags were never officially imported into Canada, although we believe a handful were brought in by some dealers; yet, currently, there are approximately three dozen in enthusiasts' hands in Ontario alone, and that number is growing by two or three examples each year.
(Courtesy Tony Fox)

Magazines and books
British Leyland Repair Operations Manual

Haynes repair manual

Illustrated Triumph Buyer's Guide
Richard Newton

Original Triumph Stag, Restorer's Guide
James Taylor

Practical Classics & Car Restorer – Triumph Stag Restoration
Kelsey Publishing

Triumph Stag
Osprey, Andrew Moreland

Triumph Stag, 1970-1977
Haynes, James Taylor

Triumph Stag, 1970-1980
Brooklands Books, R M Clarke

Triumph Stag, 1970-1984
Brooklands Books, R M Clarke

Triumph Stag, Gold Portfolio
Brooklands Books

Triumph Stag – Super Profile
Haynes, James Taylor

Triumph Stag, The Complete History
James Taylor and Dave Jell

Triumph World Magazine

DVD
Code Name Stag, Michelotti's Masterpiece
J Clancy Production

Websites
SOC www.stag.org.uk
Stag Digest www.digest.net/stag
Stag Phorum
www.triumphstag.net/start/phorum
Stag Register www.tristagreg.org
Triumph Stag Net www.triumphstag.net
TSC USA www.triumphstagclubusa.org

Parts suppliers
Abinger Hammer Motors
01306 730427
Aldridges 01902 427474
BoScreen
myweb.tiscali.co.uk/cfereday/index.htm
Brian Turner 01622 884302
E J Ward www.ejward.co.uk
Enginuity 020 8993 7737
Faversham Classics
www.favershamclassics.co.uk
James Paddock
www.jamespaddock.co.uk
LD Parts www.ldpart.co.uk
Monarch www.monarch-stags.co.uk
Rimmer Bros www.rimmerbros.co.uk
Robsports International
www.robsport.co.uk
SOC Spares Ltd 01580 292 828
Stag Parts USA
www.triumphstagpartsusa.com
Tony Hart 020 8426 1327

17 Vital statistics
– essential data at your fingertips

MkI   1970 to 1973
MkII   1973 to 1977, USA 1973 only

Federal Commission plates started with LE, non-Federal plates with LD

Total produced   **25,939**

Dimensions
Weight   2981lb including hardtop
Overall length   183.75in (4420mm)
Overall width   63.5in (1612mm)
Wheelbase   100in (2540mm)

Options
Hardtop, soft top or both
Wire wheels, steel, later alloy mags
4-speed manual with overdrive option
Borg Warner 3-speed automatic
Air-conditioning
Tinted glass
33 colours
Headrests

Specifications
Engine   2997cc, 90-degree V8
Power   145bhp (127bhp NA)
Final drive   3.70:1
Steering   Power assisted rack-and-pinion
Tyres   185 HR 14
Brakes   Disc/drum with power assist
Wheels   14in, 5.5J rim
Max speed (with overdrive) 120mph

First built   LD 1   RRW 97H
Last built   June 1977   BOL 88V

MkI and MkII differences
Engine compression ratio
Side coachline added
Instruments and backlighting revised
Seats modified
Console light added
Glovebox maplight deleted
Interior courtesy light moved from B-pillars to T-bar

Rear registration plate lights moved from the bumper to the boot lid
Alloy wheels added
Cooling system revised to sealed radiator with pressurised expansion bottle
Cooling system pressure revised from 13psi to 20psi
Door locks and linkage revised
Emblems changed to black background
Soft top rear window changed from three windows to one
16in to 14½in diameter steering wheel
Parking light position on master light switch deleted
Left footrest added
Steering rack ratio changed
Borg Warner 65 auto transmission fitted 1976
Charging system revised to alternator with built-in controls
Engine air intake revised
Bright sill finisher revised
Overdrive changed to J-type and made standard
Laminated windscreen added
Front seatback rest redesigned
Inertia-type rear seatbelts revision
Matt black tail panel added, later rescinded
Soft top liner change to beige
Matt black sills added
Small bore exhaust tail pipes adopted
Triumph emblem plinth on rear bumper made smaller
Hard and soft tops become standard
Windscreen wipers revised

Federal specification differences
Standard tinted glass
Emissions equipment includes vapour recovery system
Compression ratio and horsepower lower
Polished aluminium sill covers standard
Side marker lights, amber front and red rear
Front turn lights combined with side lights
Sealed beam headlights
Seat buzzer for ignition included
Chrome wire wheels
NA front registration plate holder
Built in front seat headrests
Stag badge added on rear wing